Desensitizing and Reprocessing:
A primer to integration

Desensitizing and Reprocessing:
A primer to integration

Dustin Cunningham

We cannot see the true nature of anything outside ourselves. Everything passes through the filter of our perception and is imprinted with our beliefs and biases automatically while our brain tries to understand what is being witnessed. It seems that what is revealed more is the true nature of the viewer that the nature of what is being viewed. Does that mean I am a bad person if I see bad people everywhere? At least that I believe I am a bad person and I do. I don't want to. And the sunset, I think I'm done.

My mom couldn't give me what I needed, a mom
I was alone without the support I needed
And I knew it
I saw what my dad was doing
I thought he was helping
I thought he was doing what he was supposed to
I started acting the same way
I didn't know what else to do
I kept trying to help her
To take away all the hurt
I put it all on myself
Hoping that if I hurt enough
If I took enough of the pain
I could free her
And I could have the mom I needed
All I got was hurt
Not a mom
Regardless of what I did
My mom never showed up
No "It's okay, mom's here now"
She wasn't and it wasn't okay

Deep inside is where I'll start from
Trying to find where
Everywhere

I just have to feel it all the way through
Take a moment
A deep slow breath
Let it all come
Try not to hold it in onto it
Let it find its own way
How does it feel so empty
And also like it's crushing me
Not crushing
Is it trying to free it's self
From my attempt to control it
Free it's self from me
Where I told it
No
Where I told it
It was bad
That's where I hid all of me
In the bad
And it's still there
I think I am the crushing feeling
Not the sad
I keep pushing it down
Because I believed them
Because I believed you
Because feelings are bad
I made them
I must be bad too
Look how you hurt everyone
I can see them
And how bad I was
Crush you
No more sad
Not more bad
Not easy not done
It won't turn off
Won't die
Won't hide from me
Why won't this bad go away...

Clench down and don't make a sound
Silence?
I still hear it
Feel it
Turing to hate
What's so wrong with me
I keep making more of this nasty thing
This sad
This bad
I don't want to be left all alone
By myself with myself
I don't know what to do
Hide more
More shadows
Crushing
Hate
I can't take anymore
I want
Something new
Or forgotten
What could happen
If I believed in myself
Instead of you
Fear
What if
It was never actually bad

I needed my mom
She wasn't there
And they told me I needed to be a good boy
for her to come back
I tried
I tried so hard
No matter what I did
I wasn't good enough
She never came back
I just sat there
Alone
Knowing I wasn't good enough to have a mom
Love me
No one held me
And told me it was okay
I held myself in a violent grasp
I knew it wasn't okay
And I knew it was because I was a monster
I caused all this
He was dead because of me
I sat and watched him die
Then sat and watched myself die

It's tricky because
As you get the pen
Close to the shadows
They run from it
As long as I chase them
They still run away

Very often, when I attempt to speak about my trauma, or anything really, I enter into a triggered state. In this triggered state my body replaces (replicates) the pattern of my historical trauma and my historical pattern. I responded to it worse. These experiences are incredibly uncomfortable and often actually damaging to my process, self-esteem, and sense of self. As was the case in my childhood, my go to response in the situation is "fawning". I don't believe anyone notices this change of consciousness I have experienced. From the outsider's perspective, when I am in this dis-regulated state, I am calm, peaceful, compliant, empathetic and compassionate. The outside world not only approves of but encourages me to act this way. As society reinforces my behaving in this manner, the cognitive result is continued conformation from these interactions that I should, as I did as a child, be quiet, agreeable, and compliant while being abused. These experiences result in both my thinking brain and my neurological brain getting to practice this pattern of response to abuse and receive conformation from the outside world that this pattern is appropriate and good.

But on the inside, my experience is much different in these exchanges. I am not always aware of exactly what the interaction was that initiated the dis-regulation, but I have gotten good at identifying when I am beginning to dis-regulate. I have not been able to reliably re-regulate myself at this point in the process. My awareness of my dis-regulation, and my awareness of my effectiveness at managing it often leads to a larger level of fear, as a helplessly witness as I lose control of my actions and behaviors. At this point, feeling helpless, powerless, and afraid, my patterned response is to attempt to keep myself safe by fawning, people pleasing. While operating in this program, my sole focus for surviving is on doing

12

whatever I can that I think will make the "threat" no longer be a threat. Since my focus is solely on the need of individuals outside myself at this point, I am unable to advocate for and protect myself. In this state, I have differed all power to those outside of me. This leaves me vulnerable to many negative outcomes. That leaves me open to being abused and exploited. It leaves me unable to scrutinize the opinions and perspectives of others, as if they were a true reflection of my own experience. It leaves me unable to openly share my opinions, perspectives, and beliefs with others, this is not only harmful to my interpersonal relationships, but also my ability to receive adequate and appropriate medical care.

There is a large amount of cognitive dissonance that is created in this as well. I am conscious and aware of my own, inner self, and with it my perspective, beliefs and needs. I am also conscious that I often communicate a message, contrary to my own beliefs, when I attempt to share them outside my own inner world. I can witness my inability to properly communicate in these moments, I often feel a large amount of frustration and anger towards myself as a result. I am frustrated and angry with myself, because I can witness myself acting in ways that I know are not true to who I am, but this far I have found myself powerless to effect any meaningful change to this dynamic.

Even though it may be dark and unknown
It is there
Waiting for me to step into it
Trust in it
Trust in me
In my feelings
My knowing
My healing
My growing
My life
My love
My choice
My voice

I want to run away
Maybe so I couldn't be found
Looking for quiet
Looking for space
Looking for peace
And running from it too
So afraid of the moment
I'm hardly there
Always running away
Funny enough
Usually
To the least safe place I've found
Abused and tormented
Writhing in the pain and shame
I did my best to keep anyone from finding it
Especially me
I know I'm the biggest traitor of all
I've watched myself do it
Since I was small
But I did find this hidden place
And I found it was in me
In it I found where my voice was trapped
Crushed smothered locked in chains
I know you are afraid of what I will do
There is no other option
Than to set it free for you

Inventory of agreements
I am bad
I am the problem
I can't talk about the problem
I can't ask for help
I don't get help
She matters more than me
I just don't matter
I can't protect myself
If I try, they will hurt me more
I can't take anymore

Act like a man
But I am a boy
Can someone show me how
I have tried
But I don't understand
I was taught men don't cry
But I feel sad all the time
I was taught men are tough and assertive
But I feel week and afraid
I was taught men stand up tall
But I feel so small
I was taught men are violent and loud
But I feel peaceful and quiet
I was taught to pull up my bootstraps
But the shoes just won't fit
I wanted to be a man
Just not like this

I told you about the place I found
Remember?
The one where you hid our voice
I know you are mad
I love you no matter what
It's okay you are mad
I betrayed us
Again
I understand why you are mad
and you can stay mad as long as you need to
I want to tell you something else
And I think you will like it
It will keep us safe
And help us heal
Learn and grow
It's a new way of looking at it
A new way to use it
Listen
Before it worked
It worked really well
But it hurt us in the way it needed
This won't hurt us
I know
It's scary for me too
Because it will help us
And that's what I'm not supposed to do
But I am
I am
Helping us
Protecting us
I am

In the wilderness (Christmas day 2023)

I know it's the best present
Even if loss was the cost
I had to lose everything
See if there's anything else
I can't take care of me
I thought that I couldn't at all
But when I listened to myself
Not what the world wants
I found all the love inside
I thought I couldn't have
Little own make
I wrapped myself up in it
In a place the world won't find
Not locked away
But protected and safe
For me to share with
The world as I wish

I saw her waiting
Confidant in her place
Not worried
He would show up
She knows
And he does
Always
She didn't ask
He just knew
A spark of magic
Excitement passion
And tension
He rushed to her
Driven by desire
For one touch
Before she slipped
Again into shadow
Drifting they both know
The moment is done
And where she must go
He still reached out
With all his strength
To touch his love
And feel her love too
I saw him start to cry
The moment he realized
She was no longer in the sky

I wanted to let you know about this morning. I woke up and immediately felt a lot of pain. Physical and emotional pain. As I focused, it started to overwhelm me. And I felt the terror start all the sudden. And I started running back and forth across my house, trying to run somewhere safe. But like always, everywhere I turned, felt no better. Something different happened though. And before my brain turned off, I sat myself down and gave myself a hug. I told myself that I was going to be there, for me. I told myself that I loved me. And I told myself that everything was gonna be OK.

The pain did not go away. But the terror did. The terror I have always felt, and the terror that I am not enough to be loved. I will wake up and everyone will be gone. And I will be all alone. All that was gone.

Because I wasn't alone. I stayed there. I tried to do all the good things I like. Do the things that I know can make me feel safer. I took a cool shower, that helped. I watched the sunrise, I really liked that. I wrote a poem and cried, that hurt but helped. I fed myself, that felt good.

I'm really sad still. But glad I'm not alone anymore.

She was beautiful
Only halfway there
Might be the best chance
They ever might have
Reaching out so hard
Might have pushed her down
And watched her fall
Tried
But couldn't help at all
Actually think
Made it worse

Focusing on the moment
Breathing it in
Letting it go
Just feeling it
With every sense
This moment feels good
Washing over me
I feel free
Exploring the pleasure
In this moment
It is everywhere
Breathing it in
Letting it go
It is right here
It is right now
In this moment is where I find
My life
Breathing it in
Letting it go

At first morning's light
I call you out
I challenge your reign
I know your power
I know where it ends
I've watched
I've felt
The pain deep inside
Felt my will defeated
I know you the same
I have changed
Left to die
After you were done
Your hatred gave me the choice
Your hatred gifted me my freedom
I choose defiance
Left nothing of you holding true
You have no power
Never did
I gave you the power
My power
I have taken it back
Alone I stand
Where is my foe today
Where is my fear today
Impotent and quelled
Unarmed and unable
I won't walk away
I know who you are
I know why you were made
I see how hard you tried
To protect us
I love you for it
As I have changed so have you
I have created a new system
I will teach it to you
You have changed
No longer will you hide it…

Now you will pull it into the light
You will run toward it
Embrace it
Love it
The pain you created is no more
Your action creates light
We will play in the light
Dance in reverie
Sing for no reason
Your action is the joy I bathe in
Your action will be truth
I will ripple across infinity
And you will have to go
Our action will change you
Forever
What you always wanted to be
Love
Hold my hand it's time to go

I'm ready to get lost
Let go of expectation
Let go of control
All of the stuff
My ego holds on
Wonder toward
Whatever makes
My heart shine
Sharing my own light
Making the love
One day at a time
Shine

I know the answer

More than a few
Days ago
I stopped dancing
Shaking now
Why did I stop
Shame from
In between my legs
Whispers and yelling
The boys and girls

Embrace truth
Hold your
Space
I hold my space   Yourself
I hold myself   Know your
I know my truth   Truth
I am love   Love
I am free   Freedom

I have fear that I am not enough to be loved for who I am. I have fear that no one cares who I am. I have fear that I will always be alone. I have fear that I need to change into something that hurts me to be attached. I have fear if I change no one will see me anyway and I will never be loved how I want to be loved. I have resentment for how shitty my childhood was because I have fear that I can't be loved because of it. I release these fears and resentments back to the universe. I know these fears and resentments are gone and hold no power over me. I know I am free. I know I am love, loving and loved. I know that the beautiful life I seek is all around me. I see that beauty and my life is filled with joy. I know that I am enough always. I know it is done. So it is.

I see it all
My life
Your life
Our life
Our everything
And nothing
Balanced
In love
Only love
Always perfect
Always growing
Moving forward
Creating love everyday

I'm not going to quit
I'm not going to run away
I'm not going to break it
I'm not going to hurt anyone
I'm going to keep trying
I'm going to stay
I'm going to create something good
I'm going to trust and grow
It's okay Dustin no matter what I will never leave you I
Will always love you
I will always Trust
Be there And
To help Listen
You protect And
You teach Talk
You hold Honest
You Love
I take the pain and use it as fuel
As energy
As instructions
Guidance
I change it to joy
Use it to create the life I want

I'm not okay today
I made some choices
And I hurt myself
And I hurt someone else
I don't want to live
In all this pain
AHHHHH
I'm sorry
I'm trying to not hate me
And I'm struggling
I hate the things I do
I hate always being scared
I hate feeling alone
But I don't hate me
I don't want to hurt anyone

I want to touch someone
Feel a tremble
Pause and relief
Excited and soothed
That I have seen their good
Trusting me to expose it all
Allowing me in
To love every piece
I want someone to touch me
Holding me in letting me know
It is safe to let go

Just keep holding
Until I can breathe again
Please don't let go of me
Until I can breathe

Today is a beautiful day
Beautiful world beautiful life
I know I am part of that beauty
I use my energy to serve the highest good
I am supported with everything I need on my path
Everything is just so in place
Always as good as it can be
I am so grateful to know this
To feel this
To live this
And so it is

I wanted to talk to you about love. It's a big fucking topic I know, and I don't imagine I have much more to offer than a scratch on the surface. But I've been looking really hard at myself and love. What it has meant to me.

What I realized is I didn't actually know what it meant to me. When I was growing up, no one ever showed me healthy love. I never saw my parents acting in a healthy loving way. Neither of them showed healthy love to me either. The relationship dynamics I witnessed were based on physical abuse, emotional abuse, threats, neglect, manipulation, deceit, dishonesty and fear and that was the extent of what I was taught to do. That's what love was in my family.

I took this understanding of love and relationships out into the real world and immediately knew it didn't feel right. And in my trying to find something that feels right or at least better. I changed to focus of my energy to sex. When I first started connecting with women in a sexual way, I was absolutely overwhelmed with how good it felt. It was the exact opposite of the pain and suffering that I thought was the limit of my reality. It opened up a whole new world of possibility to the range of experiences I could have. It, for the first time, really let me feel peace and joy.

When I witnessed this contrast, I made some assumptions. I assumed that that feeling I was experiencing was itself love. I knew that it was what I had been missing from my life, love. So I started perusing it. And initially did find it very satisfying and fulfilling my desire for love. I suppose I knew all along. It wasn't actually love. And as time has gone on, I have found it harder and harder to convince myself that it is the same thing. I see more and more how that misunderstanding keeps causing me more pain.

36

I'm working to understand and untangle all this love/sex/attachment stuff. I understand that all these things are really human needs, and I deserve to have them met. So does everyone else.

The part, I am really excited about now, despite any anxiety, I might feel toward it. Is that now I get to redefine all of those things for myself. I get to redefine them in the most beautiful and healthy ways. It is really exciting that I have the power to make this change, and it's kind of scary that it is only in my hands.

But like we have already talked about. I'm not letting fear make these decisions anymore. As I am discovering what love is to me, I am thinking more and more that love is actually what should be making these decisions.

It's weird right now
I think it feel worse
Like it's getting worse
Because I'm looking at it right now
For the first time
The shadow that followed me
Wherever I ran
Too afraid to even look
I know it's better
Even if it hurts
I did look back and see
This whole time
I have been running away from 7 year old me
I did that to me
What am I going to do now
Every time I'm afraid
Is turn around
And give him a hug
For as long as it takes
I'm not going away

Today is a day for life
For living
Today I live for him
He couldn't

I want to look at it all
Make it right
Sometimes my fear just holds on
So tight
My mind says let go
My body all it knows
Hold onto the past
Even as it stops the flow
I tried telling my body it was right
I saw that it turned my fear into fight
I saw that it couldn't listen
Because that's been the story all along
I find balance in the middle
Honoring the pain
And the future I want the same
The way forward
I have also found
My body holding
Deep in my heart
Lies my art
It's a weird squiggly path
And the only one that feels right

I don't want to be alone
But everyone scares me
I feel so stuck
Too much
Can't do it
Not today
Running away
Maybe I'll come back after a break
But by then it's usually too late
The thing I craved to love
Have turned to hate
Really focusing on me
And all the things I break
Another time around the circle
Another hole in my heart
It's up to me
To end this thing I didn't start
Understand love and be free
I don't want to be alone
But everyone is scared of me

On the edge I stand
Feeling old from the past
The new from the future
What I thought my friends
Some will get left behind
I think they all got me through
What will I do
Without Terror
Without Fear
Screaming always in my ear
What will I find
Where hate used to live
I feel uneasy
I decide
I move forward
I stand
Free
To be me
To make me
What I choose
Love

I speak
The truth
Shine A light
So bright
No hate can hide
No silence no fear
The light reveals only
Understanding peace and love

I can see
You can't deal
With your own feelings
Cowardly you put it on me
I will be the strength you don't have
I am the love you can't show

I get really
Upset that
What society
Has told me
About me
They are
Wrong
It is reasonable
For me to be
Upset
I have been mistreated
And I am
Mad
About
It

In the shadows
All the way down
Where you told me I was ugly
All the way down
Where you told me I was bad
All the way down
Where I have been frightened to look
All the way down
Where you told me you hated me
All the way down
Where you put your pain in me
All the way down
I sit learning now
All the way down
Where I found all your lies
All the way down
Where it hurts the most
All the way down
Where I found how to love myself
In the shadows

So familiar
This fear
To speak
My truth
My body
Still remembers
Being hurt
Into submission
Lies and Submission
Bound and restrained
Labeled love
This feeling
Is fear
So strong
So persuasive
Urging more
Silence and pain
But I will not
Any longer
Ignore truth
Deny myself
My voice
My freedom
My love

I will find you in the shadows
Reunited I am whole

Shining bright
The darkness vanishes
Light exposes reveals heals

Light they say, is the absolute fastest thing. The speed of everything is governed by it, it is the limit. I'm certainly not a physicist with my simple observations I'm not certain that this it the truth.

From my perception, when I look out into the universe, it seems that light is actually chasing the darkness. Wherever the light is shining, darkness was already there first. It also seems, looking into the sky at night that there is far more darkness that there is light.

Another interesting thing. There must be energy put into the system for light to be created. Darkness does not seem to require energy or effort to exist. It just simply exists, and continues to do so indefinitely. Until light shows up that is.

When the light shows up, it meets the darkness where it already exists. It does not destroy, banish or harm the darkness in any way. It appears to share the space. Wherever we find light, we find shadows as well. There is a playful dance, a give and take between the light in the dark. Light doesn't seem oppositional to darkness, but complementary.

When the light shows up, it brings some warmth, where there was only cold. It illuminates what could not be seen in the dark. It brings a chance for life, where there was none. A chance. Because without energy, there is no action, no light. With a simple veil the light can be stopped. Even with what seems like limitations, the light always seems to create the perfect balance.

The darkness already there, is definite. The light needing energy to travel, it is fragile and uncertain. How does this continue to work? In balance?

We are how it works. I believe that is why we are here. In states of love, gratitude and appreciation, the human heart can create actual light. It takes energy, effort and intention for us to be the light. Without that effort, we are darkness, sitting and waiting, for the light.

That light we create, might make more sense if we labeled it "love". It starts inside of us, when we shine the light and give the love to ourselves, we glow. In this state, we effortlessly share that love with all. That love brings balance, warmth, peace and joy. That love mends the wounded, uplift the weak, that love provides us what we all so deeply seek, acceptance. That love and acceptance beams from us and is felt by all.

When we love ourselves, we love everyone. I love myself. I love you, my friends. I see my light shining and I know where to shine it to leverage it for the greatest good. I see your light shining and I feel the love your energy creates. I see the good you create. In this moment, I see the beauty and perfection in it all. I know that everything is always in its place, and is as good as it can be. I know that we are all perfect whole and complete.

Shine Bright!

Over the last year and a half the darkness often seemed insurmountable. I felt too tired and weak. It felt hopeless. I gave up, several times.

On Christmas Eve last year, I was in one of those places, it felt like too much. For the first time sense they were born, I was not going to be able to celebrate Christmas with my youngest two children. I hadn't spoken to them in months. And this felt like too much for me.

I left my home late in the evening to drive into the mountains. I put my gun into my glove box before I left. I didn't realize it until I had drove for an hour. I was going to kill myself. Drive into the mountains, and never come back. I couldn't manage the pain. And I just needed it to end.

The universe had other plans. As I drove, what was supposed to be a minor storm turned into a blizzard. Cars were sliding off the road, zero visibility. I attempted to continue forward on my mission. I stopped at a gas station, while there, I sat in the silence of the snow. And I cried, the hardest, most real cry I can ever remember.

I couldn't do it.

I found a warm place to stay for the evening. I met an amazing woman that evening. She gave me something I actually needed, acceptance. She didn't take anything from me, and this time I honestly didn't want her to. Even with that acceptance all the pain was still there.

I broke my sobriety of over 14 years that evening. I felt like I just needed something to help numb myself, reduce the pain enough, so I could breathe, even just for a moment. That night, that woman unbeknownst to her, helped to save my life. Thank you.

I have been completely sober for one week today. Not only from the alcohol I had begun consuming again, but also from the pot that was a staple for escaping my pain.

Without these crutches, I have been hurting a lot. I've been feeling all of the things I have been avoiding. As my brain clears, and my body recuperates, I feel it getting better. I understand. Pain is an indication of an injury that needs to be healed. As I feel this pain, I know where the love needs to go, directly into my heart.

A monster is under the bed
I love him

No it's not a demon
Not a monster
Not a boogeyman
What you see here
Is just a shadow
What you see here
Is nothing to fear
Love them
As much as you can
The dark parts
They are also
Part of you

I see god everywhere. I look on my walk. God is in every step I take, god supports me. I feel it. I do not fall. The ground holds me, lifts me, guides me. As I walk I hear the birds singing god's song, letting my body know the path is safe and good. I feel my connection, my belonging, my being a part of that same god. The same intelligent being. I feel the support I give and the support I receive are the same divine love. It is everywhere. And I know I am supported always by this infinite divine love in every right action. I know my action is part of this intelligent love. In perfect balance and harmony. This system, I know, is whole perfect and complete. And I have everything needed to be a successful integrated part of this perfect whole. I am so grateful to know that I am part of this, perfect god, this perfect system, perfect universe. So thankful to know my own perfection. To know that I am perpetually supported as the whole universe is. I release this prayer knowing it is already done, that god can take it from here and it can only work in perfect accord with infinity.

What could stop me
Stepping into destiny
Me the way I see it
The only thing that
Ever has
Nothing
To be ashamed
What
They said I believed
Every word I know
Different now different
It always was
They were wrong
I am strong
I am love
I am free
I get
To
Make
ME

Smooth sailing
I tried speaking but it was stuck
All I could think of was the pain
It was too much
You betrayed every promise ever made
I sat in that dark and tried to cry
Wanting to give up and die
Reminded of how my parents didn't even try
Understood all at once exactly why
How to live with so much pain inside
All they could do was try to survive
Sat it the darkness just like them
Just not knowing how
They didn't know and never figured it out
All of us tried the best we could
The best we can to make it out
Funny staying almost seems safe
The center of it calmer than the rest
It's an illusion or maybe a test
Safety or is it a cell
Danger or is it freedom ahead
With just a little light made by me
Just a little bit I started to see
By watching them allowed me to see
Other choices were open to me
Somewhere through this storm somewhere
Is how I become free
Somewhere beyond the pain
And the emotions I can't contain
I think I was waiting to be shown the way
Some words of encouragement
A hand of support helping me through
I think I found it
In me
And in you
It is my pain
It is also my change
Everything I've wanted and needed...

Is true
Content it's perfect right here
Also excited for a new view
I can't promise it will be safe
Or that I won't make a mistake
It's all but guaranteed
The clouds will get dark
The waves will get fierce
Those are things I choose not to fear
I choose to keep going
Until the skies are clear

Walking the line	I hate…
This balance	Ok?
Feels	I fear…
Feels all of it	Ok?
Both sides unfamiliar	I love...
Acceptance unfamiliar	Ok?
Learning	I move…
Loving	Ok?
Making	I hurt…
Who I am	Ok?
Unfamiliar	I learn…
Authentically me	Ok?
And free to be	I heal…
Unwilling to fall	Ok?
Scared to balance	I fail…
To try too hard	Ok?
Both actually okay?	I succeed…
How weird	Ok?
All that's in me okay?	Balancing…
Even the fear	Ok?
Is not knowing okay?	Yes
My choice	I am…
Letting go okay?	Ok

One love that is all that is. It is all just vibrating. All the same stuff. The stuff that actually makes stuff just by looking at it. God. And I guess I am that stuff. Looking and creating. I see it is all the same. The same vibration. I am that love. I am worthy and receive that love. Unstoppable love. I am healed and free. I create beautiful things. I am supported and guided by this one love. I travel with ease and grace as I travel through this perfect life. I feel this truth in my body in my mind and soul. I am so grateful to know this truth, I love my life. Floating down the stream, I am free. Peace and love.

I do know what I am doing
I am figuring it out
Each day
Every day
Finding my way
Making it up
Each choice I make
Every step I take
Any choice I make
Never a mistake
Always something to learn
Stay present
Stay awake
In the unknown
Finding my home
Thankful for a chance
To breath today
Thankful I don't know the way
Thankful I get to
Make today
Perfect and free
Created by me

Because
I
Believe
In
Me

All the pieces
Are
Perfect
All the
Pieces of
Me

Stuck as a kid
A kid stuck in me
Appropriately
Why won't anyone answer me
Don't understand my words
Not the right words
Some kind of context
On the missing piece
Just tell it to myself
Or the wind
Carry away
Is it really true
Circling around
Words like a hex
My tongue
My stomach
The right side of my brain
Moving from me
The words aren't there

The whole world went away
What do I do

It hurts too much
I just want it to stop
All of it to stop
Somedays
All I see
Is the pain

Soon free
No more me
No more world of shadows
I want it to all end
Please
Help
Me
Into the dark
Die die die

Feeling all the feelings
Overwhelmed
What do I call them
And what can I do
Process something unknown
Tell myself I'm ok
Never out loud
The words betray
Intention of my heart
Scrambled in my brain
I'm not
I'm not strong enough today
Misunderstood
Guided astray
No help found in the
In the words I say
Just proof I'm not human
I should stay away
Safer inside
Safer to hide
Some company and comfort
Maybe
For the little boy who died
Everyone hated him
Especially when he cried
They still do
Sometimes I still believe
And hate him too
Ashamed
Scared
Of what monsters do
Don't call him that
It's not true
How do I forget
Forgive
Make something new
Love and accept
The anger and hatred…

Overflowing from you
How do I find comfort
And say it's okay
How do I love myself
Stop making this mistake
Just keep trying
He knows it's fake
Move forward
The worlds too much to take
What can I do
To make it through today
Revive
Survive
Thrive
Maybe these words
Are enough
To keep him alive

Feeling-thought-action
Thought-feeling-action
Action-thought-feeling
Action-feeling-thought
Feeling-action-thought
Thought-action-feeling

Is remembering a thought or action?
Are all 3 needed?
Is 1 more important?
Which 1?
What about order?
Not just my action?
The worlds action?
Can they be wrong?
Only if I think so?
Does that mean I'm wrong?
Maybe it's not a line?
Is it really the same thing?
Is there choice and freedom?
Do I get to decide?
Is it bound to a law?
What is love?
All 3?
What about me?
A container?
A creator?

I can still feel you
No matter how far away
Crushing clinging
Wandering dimly lit
Still in here somewhere
I can still feel you
Still looking
Still hoping
I thought
You were gone
All of it
I wanted gone
And I tried
Keep finding more
Hiding too
I linger
Find alone
Find silence
Find peace
I can still feel you
Pieces I pull
Both me and you
I found him
Deep below
He still held you tight
Loving with all his might
Sitting in the dark
Waiting for light
Your light
I told him the truth
He let go
But really slow
And I can still feel you

There is no greater power
No power greater
Power
Power
My power
I am the power
Not in my hand
It is my hand

Thought
Will
Skill
These 3
Nothing becomes 1
Power
Pen to paper
Eye
Mouth hand
Power

I said I would always be there
I tried
But I lied
I tried
But I couldn't
I tried
But slipped away
I tried
But can't find my way back
I still try
Everyday
Patience in pain
I try
Sitting alone in the rain
Washing away
I try
To change that hate
I fail
I fall
I try
I stand
I cry
I try
Everyday

Shared perspective
Unity
Cooperation
One and 2

One thing I heard
It's safe
Over and over
The actions
Defy the words
My heart
Holds the truth
My ears
Quickly abandon
My own view
A learned response
Wanting to be good
Defiant
I don't accept
Your view
The safest place
Actually
Is opposing you
Not believing you
That is how
We create
Something new

Feel the pendulum swing
Standing in place
Holding my space
I feel the swing
Fate is a fiction
Exercise my will
Freedom in place
Rides right beside

I release all fear and resentment that I am not enough. That people will take advantage of me and that I can't stand up for myself. I have fear I am not enough; I am enough to accomplish everything I need to accomplish. I am good. Other's actions have no effect on this value. It is immutable, even by my own action. Nothing can change that I am enough.

I feel a lot
All the time
Projection
Absorption
It responds to the intensity of the feeling
All feelings are good feelings
My body holds it
Until I feel it
I have a lot to feel
People are always scarry
When I get like this
I need people
But too afraid
To let them help

I find myself fighting again
Fighting that same voice
"I hate you"
"Everyone hates you"
"You are not loveable"
I feel the hate
From everywhere
Fear filled heart
A rotten hole in my chest
Rotten
Worthless helpless
And unhelpable
A word
A belief
I believed
I believe
Now
What she told me
Only her view
I believed it enough
I made it true
It feels right
The suffering inside
Telling the story
Helping myself
Letting go
Healing the pain
Feels worse sometimes
Betraying the ones
That gave me the shame
This name
Not a belief
But a thought
A start
I can do something new
Whatever I can
Cover all those broken pieces
In love and compassion…

Every time I do succeed
I start to believe
Little by little
I might be enough
Just the way I am
Peace and love
Are in me now

Underneath the waves
There is still love
Despite the turbulence
The chaos and struggle
The pain
I hold it at my center
And I don't know
How to let go
My brain just stops
All it can hear
That deafening scream
Coming from near
Too loud
And too proud
Bringing back to fear
I breath and I center
I ground and prepare
For another day
Without you here

Where do the shadows meet?
Of course
And where is it

           And it changes

But it is magic there?

           I don't know

…

           Must

You have seen

           Never

…

           Felt
           Feel

And it changes

           In your heart

    Everything changes

I can't fit
No I won't fit
I won't squeeze
I won't stuff
I won't shove
Myself into
The hole
You created
For me
It was
Never for me
That hole
Is your
Grave
Digging
Your whole life
Trying to hide
Pain inside
Look strong
Telling lies
Pass it on
To me
Or anyone
Holding more
Strength
Then you
You can stay
In the ruin
I've found a new way
New words to say
A much better
Game to play
No violence
No lies
No blame
No shame
No fear
Now your voice…

Isn't here
It's a game
Of love
Loving life
Loving me
Loving free
In my game
Everyone wins
Is heard
Is seen
No deceit
All clean
I'll be waiting
Right here
In case
You decide
You don't
Want to be mean

Let there be light
Is darkness necessary to perceive light
What was it I needed to calm down?

Published by Dustin Makes LLC
Colorado Springs, CO, USA
Dustincunningham.art

Cover design by: Dora Haslinger

ISBN: 979-8-9929442-0-4

Library of congress control number: 2025909209